What Is Letter Hunting?

The great typographer Rudolph Koch once said that "the making of letters in every form is for me the purest and the greatest pleasure, and at many stages of my life it was to me what a song is to the singer, a picture to the painter, a shout to the elated, or a sign to the oppressed." This notebook is all about making letters, and enjoying and being inspired by the "letter songs" that others have made previous to you.

Inspiration can come from anywhere, but whether you're a typographer, an artist, or just an enthusiast of good design, sometimes you have to take a walk and see what's out there. That's where letter hunting comes in. In a world driven by letters and language—signage, advertising, wayfinding signs, corporate logos, graffiti, high art and low—simply viewing and recording the great typography that surrounds you can generate instant inspiration and creative excitement. We, and many others, have been doing this for years on social media, with the hashtag #letterhunt (and similar hashtags): see an amazing sign or letterform, take a photo, hashtag, and post. It's a quick, easy way to turn something as mundane as even your morning commute into a typographic expedition.

So what if we took it one step further? This notebook is the analog, nuts-and-bolts version of the #letterhunt hashtag. It's a place to record, sketch, and riff off of the letters that, like Koch says, brings you the purest and greatest pleasure.

There's no right way to use this journal. Fill it with notes and doodles, draw and sketch on every page—it's up to you. We do, however, provide a few loose ways for you to record the date, location, and type of letterform you're admiring on your expeditions so that as the journal fills up, you have created a historical record of not only your local typographic neighborhood but also your own creative process. However you use it, let it be a way for you to look for the unexpected, and find inspiration in every and any thing you encounter with your eyes wide open.

Happy hunting!

LOCATION _____ DATE _____

CLASSIFICATION
- ◯ SERIF
- ◯ SANS SERIF
- ◯ SCRIPT
- ◯ SYMBOL

- ◯ DECORATIVE
- ◯ ROUNDED
- ◯ HAND LETTERED
- ◯ OTHER

IMPLEMENTATION
- ◯ PAINTED
- ◯ CARVED
- ◯ RELIEF
- ◯ DIMENSIONAL

- ◯ STONE
- ◯ WOOD
- ◯ PLASTIC
- ◯ METAL

- ◯ GLASS
- ◯ NEON
- ◯ DIGITAL
- ◯ MURAL

- ◯ BUILDING
- ◯ VEHICLE
- ◯ BILLBOARD
- ◯ OTHER

LOCATION _____ DATE _____

CLASSIFICATION
- ○ SERIF
- ○ SANS SERIF
- ○ SCRIPT
- ○ SYMBOL
- ○ DECORATIVE
- ○ ROUNDED
- ○ HAND LETTERED
- ○ OTHER

IMPLEMENTATION
- ○ PAINTED
- ○ CARVED
- ○ RELIEF
- ○ DIMENSIONAL
- ○ STONE
- ○ WOOD
- ○ PLASTIC
- ○ METAL
- ○ GLASS
- ○ NEON
- ○ DIGITAL
- ○ MURAL
- ○ BUILDING
- ○ VEHICLE
- ○ BILLBOARD
- ○ OTHER

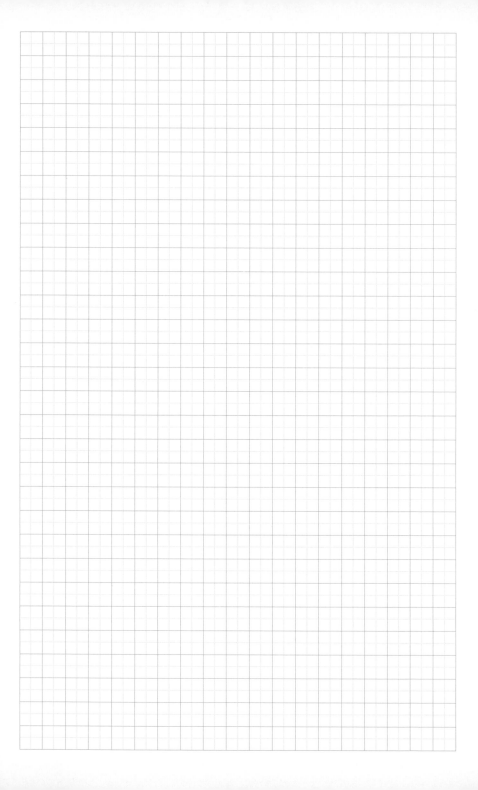

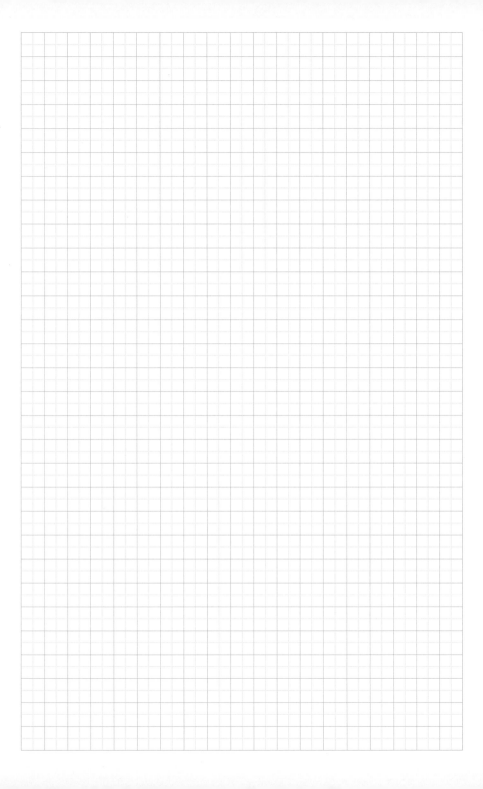

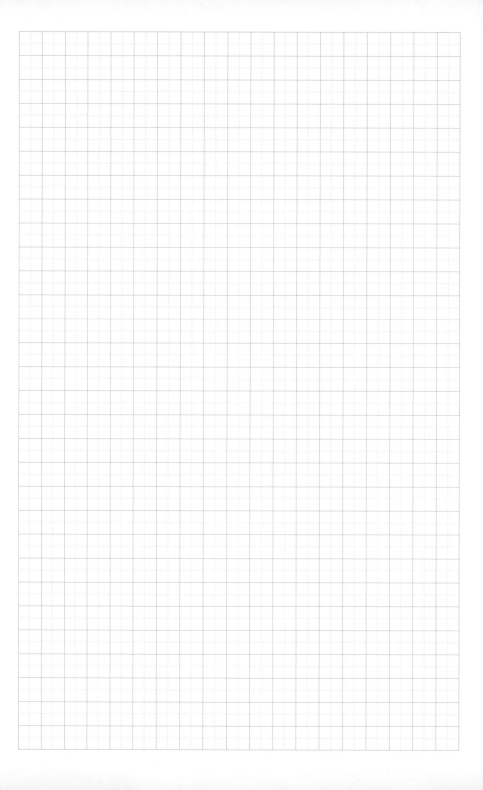

CLASSIFICATION
- ○ SERIF
- ○ SANS SERIF
- ○ SCRIPT
- ○ SYMBOL

- ○ DECORATIVE
- ○ ROUNDED
- ○ HAND LETTERED
- ○ OTHER

IMPLEMENTATION
- ○ PAINTED
- ○ CARVED
- ○ RELIEF
- ○ DIMENSIONAL

- ○ STONE
- ○ WOOD
- ○ PLASTIC
- ○ METAL

- ○ GLASS
- ○ NEON
- ○ DIGITAL
- ○ MURAL

- ○ BUILDING
- ○ VEHICLE
- ○ BILLBOARD
- ○ OTHER

LOCATION _____ DATE _____

CLASSIFICATION
- ◯ SERIF
- ◯ SANS SERIF
- ◯ SCRIPT
- ◯ SYMBOL

- ◯ DECORATIVE
- ◯ ROUNDED
- ◯ HAND LETTERED
- ◯ OTHER

IMPLEMENTATION
- ◯ PAINTED
- ◯ CARVED
- ◯ RELIEF
- ◯ DIMENSIONAL

- ◯ STONE
- ◯ WOOD
- ◯ PLASTIC
- ◯ METAL

- ◯ GLASS
- ◯ NEON
- ◯ DIGITAL
- ◯ MURAL

- ◯ BUILDING
- ◯ VEHICLE
- ◯ BILLBOARD
- ◯ OTHER

LOCATION _____ DATE _____

CLASSIFICATION
- ◯ SERIF
- ◯ SANS SERIF
- ◯ SCRIPT
- ◯ SYMBOL
- ◯ DECORATIVE
- ◯ ROUNDED
- ◯ HAND LETTERED
- ◯ OTHER

IMPLEMENTATION
- ◯ PAINTED
- ◯ CARVED
- ◯ RELIEF
- ◯ DIMENSIONAL
- ◯ STONE
- ◯ WOOD
- ◯ PLASTIC
- ◯ METAL
- ◯ GLASS
- ◯ NEON
- ◯ DIGITAL
- ◯ MURAL
- ◯ BUILDING
- ◯ VEHICLE
- ◯ BILLBOARD
- ◯ OTHER

CLASSIFICATION
- ◯ SERIF
- ◯ SANS SERIF
- ◯ SCRIPT
- ◯ SYMBOL

- ◯ DECORATIVE
- ◯ ROUNDED
- ◯ HAND LETTERED
- ◯ OTHER

IMPLEMENTATION
- ◯ PAINTED
- ◯ CARVED
- ◯ RELIEF
- ◯ DIMENSIONAL

- ◯ STONE
- ◯ WOOD
- ◯ PLASTIC
- ◯ METAL

- ◯ GLASS
- ◯ NEON
- ◯ DIGITAL
- ◯ MURAL

- ◯ BUILDING
- ◯ VEHICLE
- ◯ BILLBOARD
- ◯ OTHER

LOCATION _____ DATE _____

CLASSIFICATION
- ○ SERIF
- ○ SANS SERIF
- ○ SCRIPT
- ○ SYMBOL

- ○ DECORATIVE
- ○ ROUNDED
- ○ HAND LETTERED
- ○ OTHER

IMPLEMENTATION
- ○ PAINTED
- ○ CARVED
- ○ RELIEF
- ○ DIMENSIONAL

- ○ STONE
- ○ WOOD
- ○ PLASTIC
- ○ METAL

- ○ GLASS
- ○ NEON
- ○ DIGITAL
- ○ MURAL

- ○ BUILDING
- ○ VEHICLE
- ○ BILLBOARD
- ○ OTHER

LOCATION _____ DATE _____

- ○ SERIF
- ○ SANS SERIF
- ○ SCRIPT
- ○ SYMBOL

- ○ DECORATIVE
- ○ ROUNDED
- ○ HAND LETTERED
- ○ OTHER

- ○ PAINTED
- ○ CARVED
- ○ RELIEF
- ○ DIMENSIONAL

- ○ STONE
- ○ WOOD
- ○ PLASTIC
- ○ METAL

- ○ GLASS
- ○ NEON
- ○ DIGITAL
- ○ MURAL

- ○ BUILDING
- ○ VEHICLE
- ○ BILLBOARD
- ○ OTHER

CLASSIFICATION

- ( ) SERIF
- ( ) SANS SERIF
- ( ) SCRIPT
- ( ) SYMBOL

- ( ) DECORATIVE
- ( ) ROUNDED
- ( ) HAND LETTERED
- ( ) OTHER

IMPLEMENTATION

- ( ) PAINTED
- ( ) CARVED
- ( ) RELIEF
- ( ) DIMENSIONAL

- ( ) STONE
- ( ) WOOD
- ( ) PLASTIC
- ( ) METAL

- ( ) GLASS
- ( ) NEON
- ( ) DIGITAL
- ( ) MURAL

- ( ) BUILDING
- ( ) VEHICLE
- ( ) BILLBOARD
- ( ) OTHER

LOCATION _____ DATE _____

CLASSIFICATION
- ◯ SERIF
- ◯ SANS SERIF
- ◯ SCRIPT
- ◯ SYMBOL

- ◯ DECORATIVE
- ◯ ROUNDED
- ◯ HAND LETTERED
- ◯ OTHER

IMPLEMENTATION
- ◯ PAINTED
- ◯ CARVED
- ◯ RELIEF
- ◯ DIMENSIONAL

- ◯ STONE
- ◯ WOOD
- ◯ PLASTIC
- ◯ METAL

- ◯ GLASS
- ◯ NEON
- ◯ DIGITAL
- ◯ MURAL

- ◯ BUILDING
- ◯ VEHICLE
- ◯ BILLBOARD
- ◯ OTHER

CLASSIFICATION
- ◯ SERIF
- ◯ SANS SERIF
- ◯ SCRIPT
- ◯ SYMBOL

- ◯ DECORATIVE
- ◯ ROUNDED
- ◯ HAND LETTERED
- ◯ OTHER

IMPLEMENTATION
- ◯ PAINTED
- ◯ CARVED
- ◯ RELIEF
- ◯ DIMENSIONAL

- ◯ STONE
- ◯ WOOD
- ◯ PLASTIC
- ◯ METAL

- ◯ GLASS
- ◯ NEON
- ◯ DIGITAL
- ◯ MURAL

- ◯ BUILDING
- ◯ VEHICLE
- ◯ BILLBOARD
- ◯ OTHER

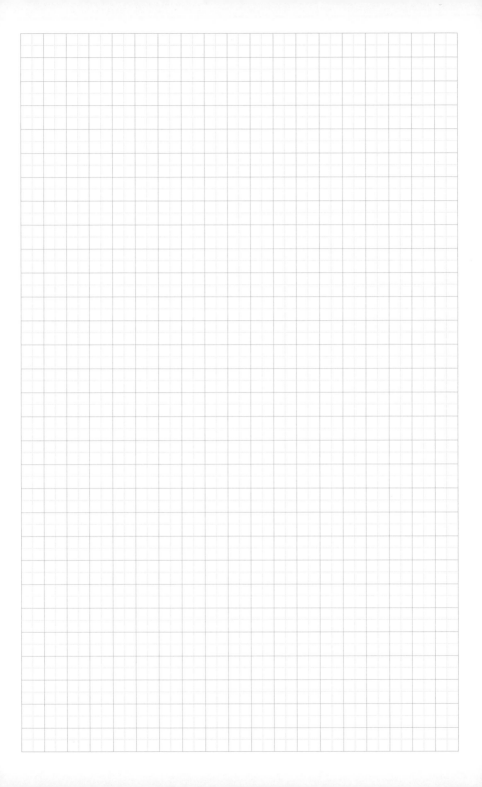

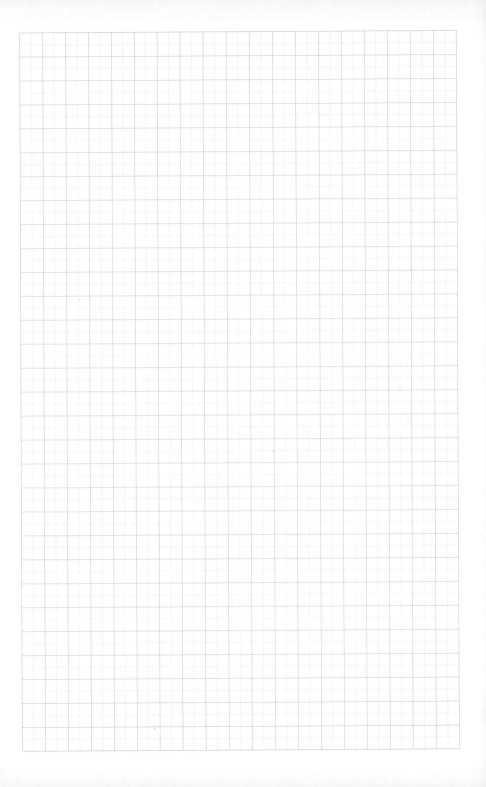

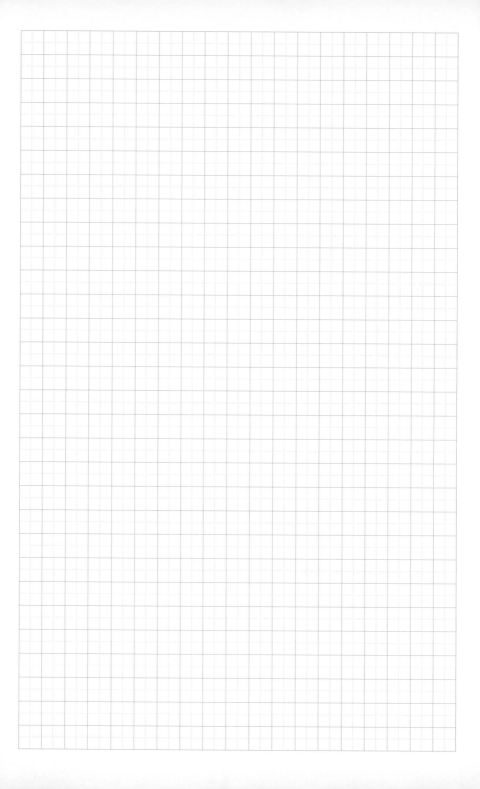

CLASSIFICATION
- ( ) SERIF
- ( ) SANS SERIF
- ( ) SCRIPT
- ( ) SYMBOL
- ( ) DECORATIVE
- ( ) ROUNDED
- ( ) HAND LETTERED
- ( ) OTHER

IMPLEMENTATION
- ( ) PAINTED
- ( ) CARVED
- ( ) RELIEF
- ( ) DIMENSIONAL
- ( ) STONE
- ( ) WOOD
- ( ) PLASTIC
- ( ) METAL
- ( ) GLASS
- ( ) NEON
- ( ) DIGITAL
- ( ) MURAL
- ( ) BUILDING
- ( ) VEHICLE
- ( ) BILLBOARD
- ( ) OTHER

LOCATION _____ DATE _____

CLASSIFICATION
- ○ SERIF
- ○ SANS SERIF
- ○ SCRIPT
- ○ SYMBOL

- ○ DECORATIVE
- ○ ROUNDED
- ○ HAND LETTERED
- ○ OTHER

IMPLEMENTATION
- ○ PAINTED
- ○ CARVED
- ○ RELIEF
- ○ DIMENSIONAL

- ○ STONE
- ○ WOOD
- ○ PLASTIC
- ○ METAL

- ○ GLASS
- ○ NEON
- ○ DIGITAL
- ○ MURAL

- ○ BUILDING
- ○ VEHICLE
- ○ BILLBOARD
- ○ OTHER

LOCATION _____ DATE _____

CLASSIFICATION

○ SERIF   ○ DECORATIVE
○ SANS SERIF   ○ ROUNDED
○ SCRIPT   ○ HAND LETTERED
○ SYMBOL   ○ OTHER

IMPLEMENTATION

○ PAINTED   ○ STONE   ○ GLASS   ○ BUILDING
○ CARVED   ○ WOOD   ○ NEON   ○ VEHICLE
○ RELIEF   ○ PLASTIC   ○ DIGITAL   ○ BILLBOARD
○ DIMENSIONAL   ○ METAL   ○ MURAL   ○ OTHER

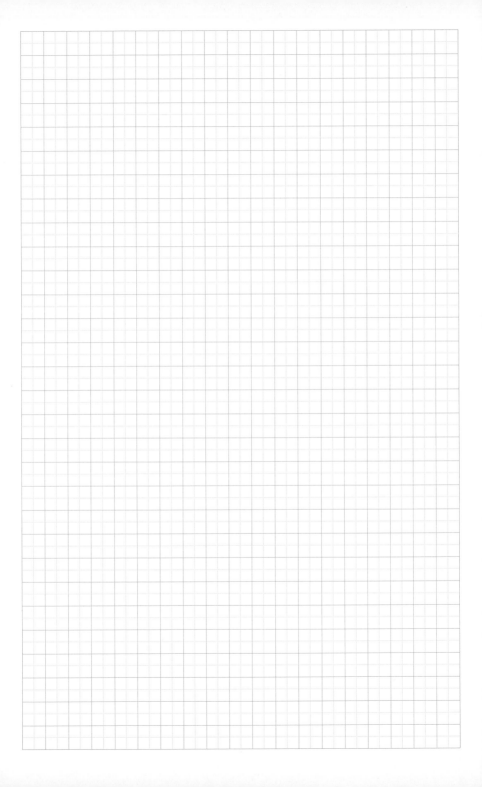

CLASSIFICATION
- ( ) SERIF
- ( ) SANS SERIF
- ( ) SCRIPT
- ( ) SYMBOL

- ( ) DECORATIVE
- ( ) ROUNDED
- ( ) HAND LETTERED
- ( ) OTHER

IMPLEMENTATION
- ( ) PAINTED
- ( ) CARVED
- ( ) RELIEF
- ( ) DIMENSIONAL

- ( ) STONE
- ( ) WOOD
- ( ) PLASTIC
- ( ) METAL

- ( ) GLASS
- ( ) NEON
- ( ) DIGITAL
- ( ) MURAL

- ( ) BUILDING
- ( ) VEHICLE
- ( ) BILLBOARD
- ( ) OTHER

LOCATION _____ DATE _____

CLASSIFICATION
- ○ SERIF
- ○ SANS SERIF
- ○ SCRIPT
- ○ SYMBOL

- ○ DECORATIVE
- ○ ROUNDED
- ○ HAND LETTERED
- ○ OTHER

IMPLEMENTATION
- ○ PAINTED
- ○ CARVED
- ○ RELIEF
- ○ DIMENSIONAL

- ○ STONE
- ○ WOOD
- ○ PLASTIC
- ○ METAL

- ○ GLASS
- ○ NEON
- ○ DIGITAL
- ○ MURAL

- ○ BUILDING
- ○ VEHICLE
- ○ BILLBOARD
- ○ OTHER

CLASSIFICATION

- ○ SERIF
- ○ SANS SERIF
- ○ SCRIPT
- ○ SYMBOL

- ○ DECORATIVE
- ○ ROUNDED
- ○ HAND LETTERED
- ○ OTHER

IMPLEMENTATION

- ○ PAINTED
- ○ CARVED
- ○ RELIEF
- ○ DIMENSIONAL

- ○ STONE
- ○ WOOD
- ○ PLASTIC
- ○ METAL

- ○ GLASS
- ○ NEON
- ○ DIGITAL
- ○ MURAL

- ○ BUILDING
- ○ VEHICLE
- ○ BILLBOARD
- ○ OTHER

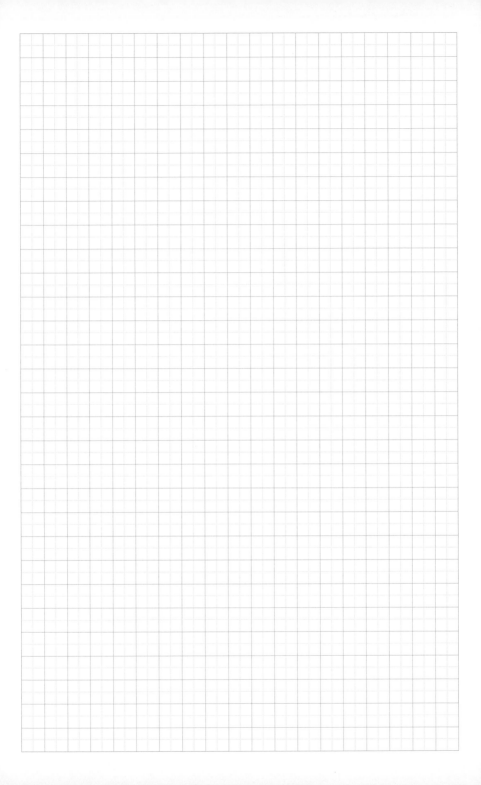

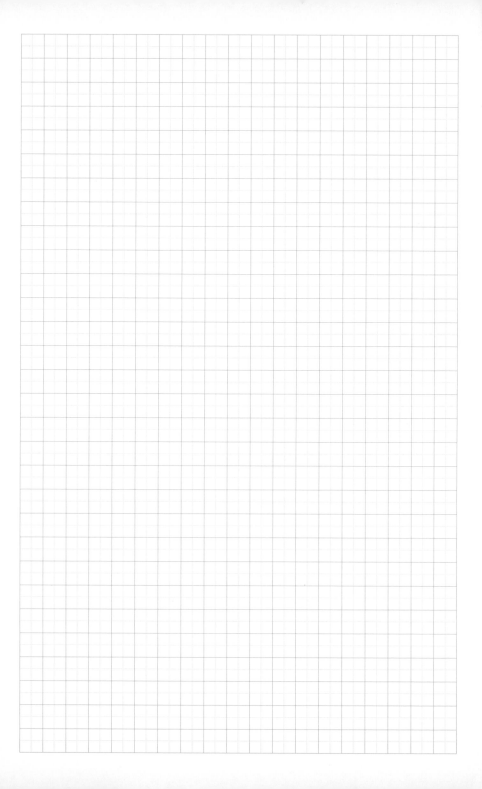

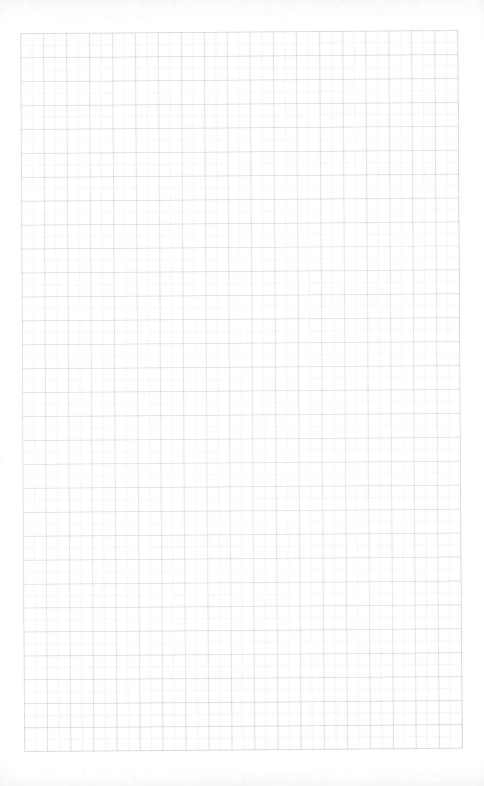

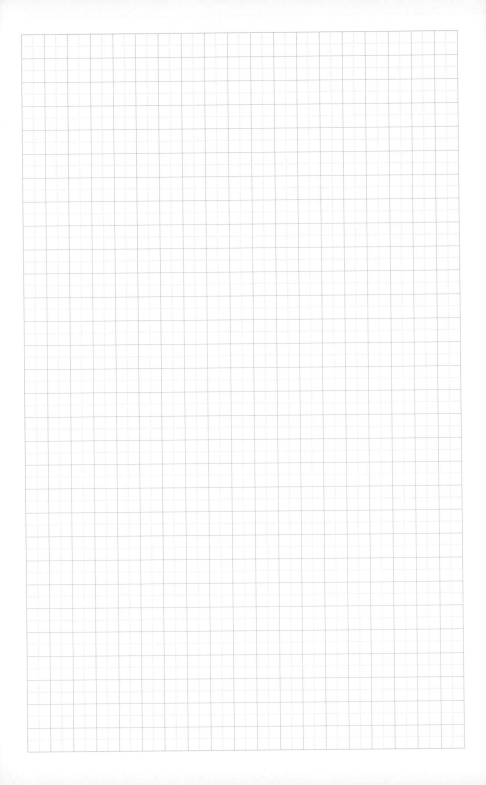

LOCATION _____ DATE _____

○ SERIF   ○ DECORATIVE   IMPLEMENTATION ○ PAINTED   ○ STONE   ○ GLASS   ○ BUILDING
○ SANS SERIF   ○ ROUNDED   ○ CARVED   ○ WOOD   ○ NEON   ○ VEHICLE
○ SCRIPT   ○ HAND LETTERED   ○ RELIEF   ○ PLASTIC   ○ DIGITAL   ○ BILLBOARD
○ SYMBOL   ○ OTHER   ○ DIMENSIONAL   ○ METAL   ○ MURAL   ○ OTHER

BKI

OPEN

YN

24 HRS.

LOCATION _____ DATE _____

CLASSIFICATION

○ SERIF   ○ DECORATIVE
○ SANS SERIF ○ ROUNDED
○ SCRIPT   ○ HAND LETTERED
○ SYMBOL   ○ OTHER

IMPLEMENTATION

○ PAINTED   ○ STONE   ○ GLASS   ○ BUILDING
○ CARVED   ○ WOOD   ○ NEON   ○ VEHICLE
○ RELIEF   ○ PLASTIC ○ DIGITAL ○ BILLBOARD
○ DIMENSIONAL ○ METAL   ○ MURAL   ○ OTHER

LOCATION _____ DATE _____

CLASSIFICATION
- ◯ SERIF
- ◯ SANS SERIF
- ◯ SCRIPT
- ◯ SYMBOL

- ◯ DECORATIVE
- ◯ ROUNDED
- ◯ HAND LETTERED
- ◯ OTHER

IMPLEMENTATION
- ◯ PAINTED
- ◯ CARVED
- ◯ RELIEF
- ◯ DIMENSIONAL

- ◯ STONE
- ◯ WOOD
- ◯ PLASTIC
- ◯ METAL

- ◯ GLASS
- ◯ NEON
- ◯ DIGITAL
- ◯ MURAL

- ◯ BUILDING
- ◯ VEHICLE
- ◯ BILLBOARD
- ◯ OTHER

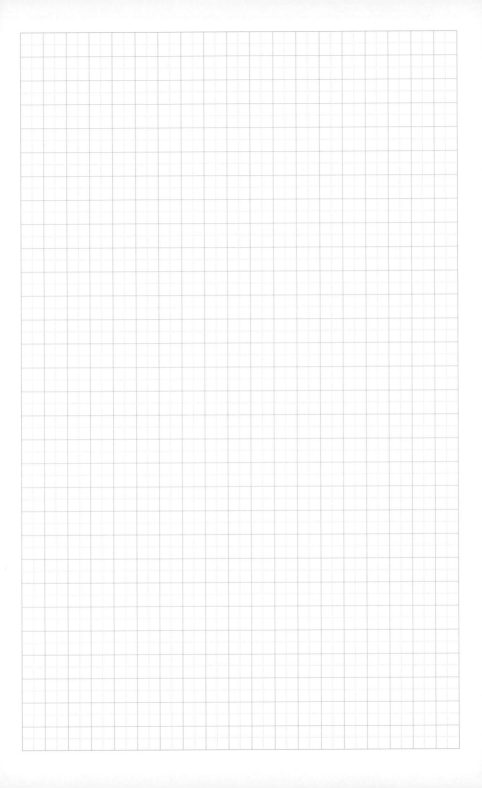

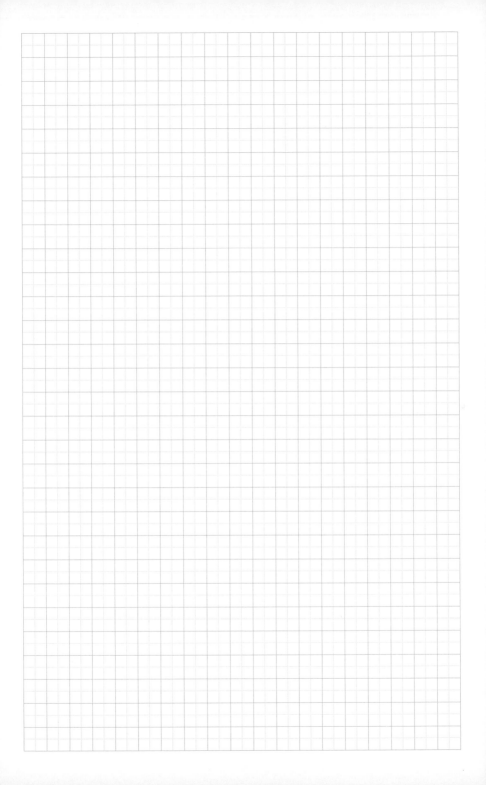

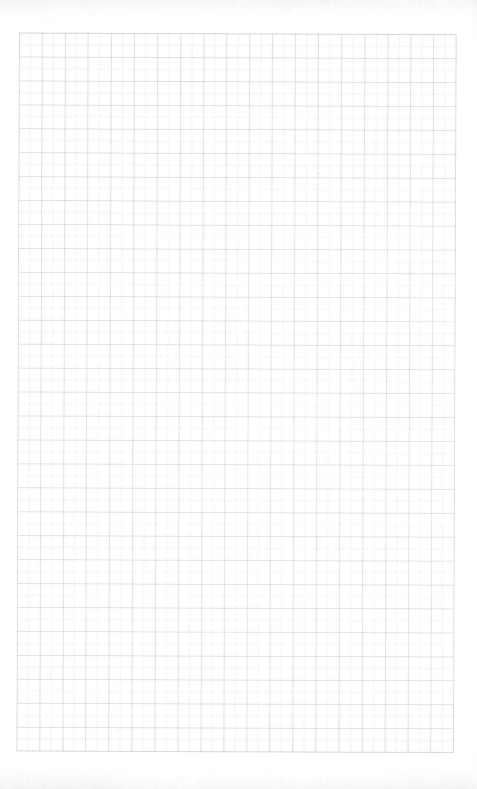

CLASSIFICATION
- ◯ SERIF
- ◯ SANS SERIF
- ◯ SCRIPT
- ◯ SYMBOL

- ◯ DECORATIVE
- ◯ ROUNDED
- ◯ HAND LETTERED
- ◯ OTHER

IMPLEMENTATION
- ◯ PAINTED
- ◯ CARVED
- ◯ RELIEF
- ◯ DIMENSIONAL

- ◯ STONE
- ◯ WOOD
- ◯ PLASTIC
- ◯ METAL

- ◯ GLASS
- ◯ NEON
- ◯ DIGITAL
- ◯ MURAL

- ◯ BUILDING
- ◯ VEHICLE
- ◯ BILLBOARD
- ◯ OTHER

The &

LOCATION _____ DATE _____

CLASSIFICATION
- ◯ SERIF
- ◯ SANS SERIF
- ◯ SCRIPT
- ◯ SYMBOL

- ◯ DECORATIVE
- ◯ ROUNDED
- ◯ HAND LETTERED
- ◯ OTHER

IMPLEMENTATION
- ◯ PAINTED
- ◯ CARVED
- ◯ RELIEF
- ◯ DIMENSIONAL

- ◯ STONE
- ◯ WOOD
- ◯ PLASTIC
- ◯ METAL

- ◯ GLASS
- ◯ NEON
- ◯ DIGITAL
- ◯ MURAL

- ◯ BUILDING
- ◯ VEHICLE
- ◯ BILLBOARD
- ◯ OTHER

CLASSIFICATION
- ( ) SERIF
- ( ) SANS SERIF
- ( ) SCRIPT
- ( ) SYMBOL
- ( ) DECORATIVE
- ( ) ROUNDED
- ( ) HAND LETTERED
- ( ) OTHER

IMPLEMENTATION
- ( ) PAINTED
- ( ) CARVED
- ( ) RELIEF
- ( ) DIMENSIONAL
- ( ) STONE
- ( ) WOOD
- ( ) PLASTIC
- ( ) METAL
- ( ) GLASS
- ( ) NEON
- ( ) DIGITAL
- ( ) MURAL
- ( ) BUILDING
- ( ) VEHICLE
- ( ) BILLBOARD
- ( ) OTHER

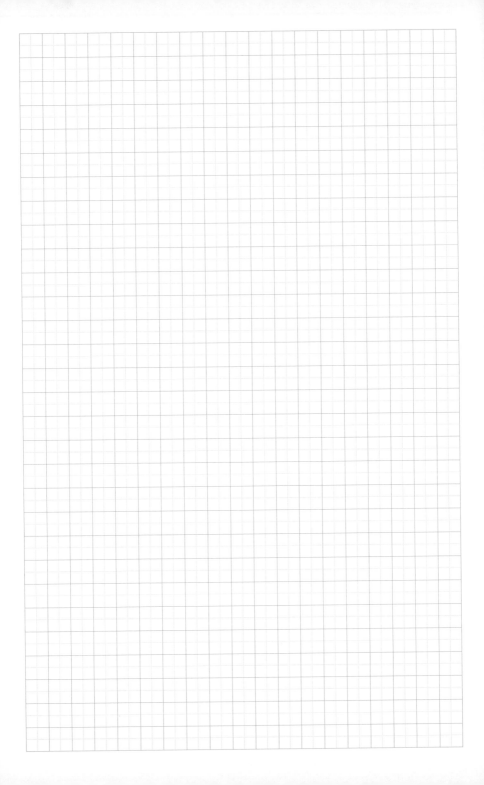

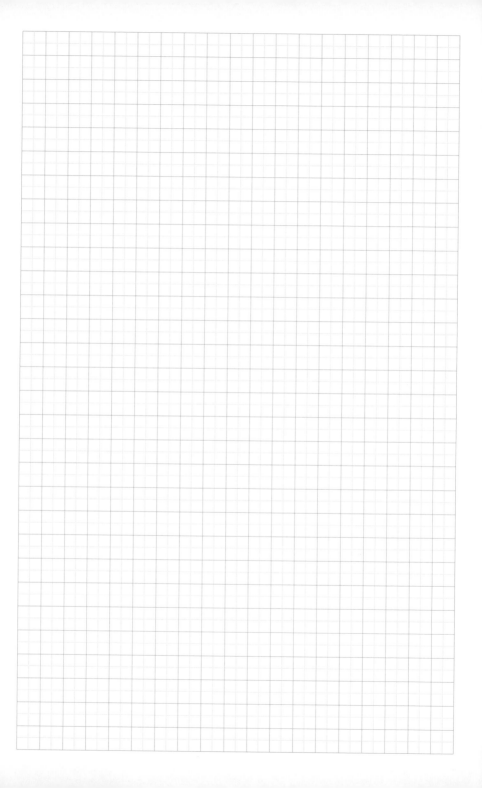

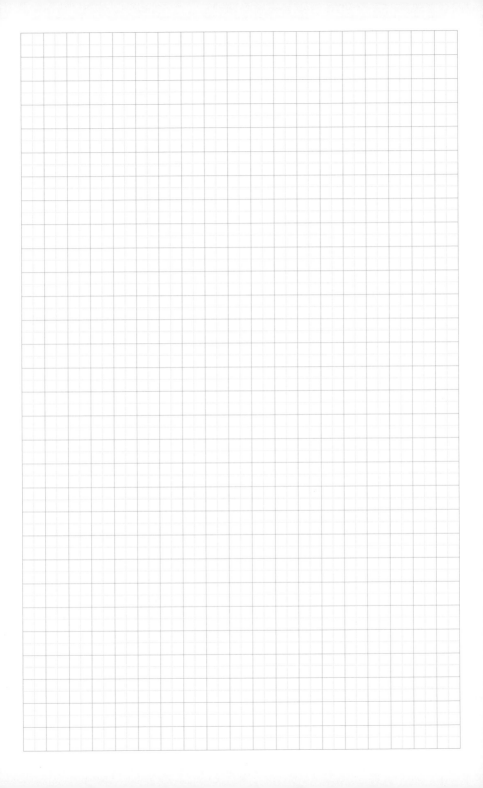

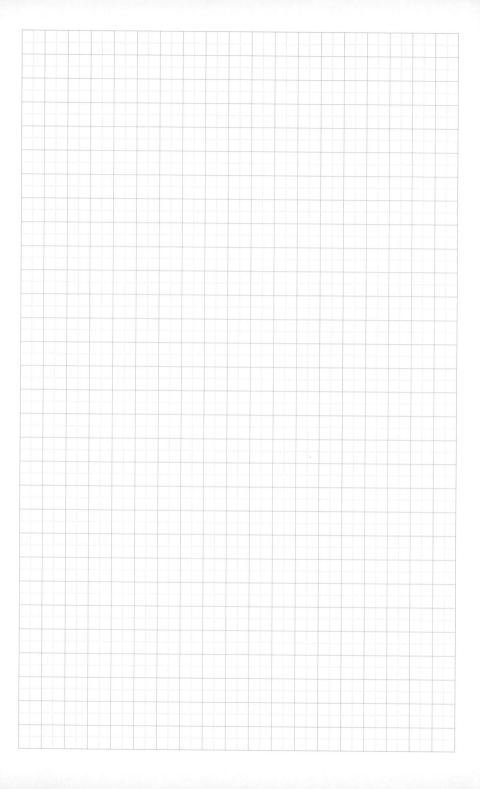

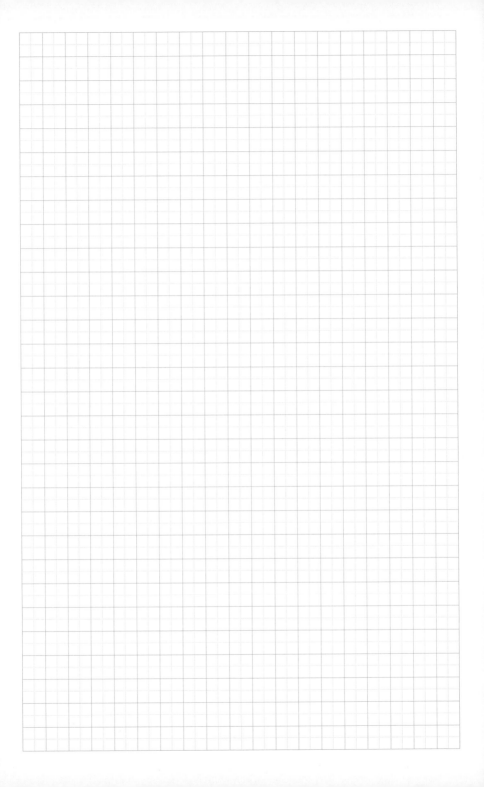

LOCATION _____ DATE _____

Anatomy of Type

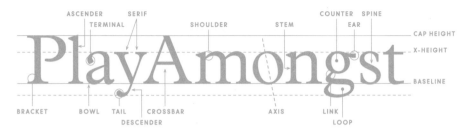

Terms

ARM/LEG: Ascending or descending (horizontal or diagonal) stroke, either connected on one end and open on the other (the left stroke of the y in Play), or free on both ends (such as in the capital letter T)

ASCENDER: Upward vertical stroke making up the part of a lowercase letterform that extends above its x-height (b, d, f, h, k, l, t)

BOWL: Fully closed, rounded stroke that encloses the curved part of a letter (found in letters like d, b, o, p)

BRACKET: Curved line connecting the serif to the stroke

CAP HEIGHT: Height of uppercase letters when measured from the baseline

COUNTER: Negative space in a letter partially or fully enclosed by a curved stroke

CROSSBAR: Horizontal bar connecting two strokes, such as in the uppercase A and H

DESCENDER: Part of a letter that extends below its baseline (in lowercase letters such as g and p, and sometimes in uppercase letters like Q and J)

EAR: Small stroke often used as a decorative flourish, found in a lowercase g or r

LINK: Stroke that connects the top and bottom parts of a lowercase double-story g

LOOP: Enclosed counter of a letterform that falls below the baseline, typically found in a double-story g; the enclosed extenders in the cursive letters like p, b, and l are also referred to as the loop

SERIF: Terminating flourish at the end of a letter's main strokes

SHOULDER: Curved stroke aiming downward from its origin at a letter's stem (h, m, n)

SPINE: Main curved stroke of a lowercase or uppercase S

SPUR: Small projection from a letter's main stroke, found in many uppercase Gs

STEM: Full-length vertical stroke in upright characters (or the main straight diagonal in a letter without verticals)

STRESS: Diagonal, vertical, or horizontal directional thickening in a letter's curved stroke

STROKE: Straight or curved line making up a letterform

SWASH: Embellishing extension on a letterform replacing a terminal or serif

TAIL: Descending, often decorative, stroke of the uppercase Q or diagonal of the K or R

TERMINAL: Straight or curved end at the end of a stroke not capped by a serif

X-HEIGHT: Height of all lowercase letters, disregarding their ascenders and descenders, typically delineated by the lowercase x in most typefaces

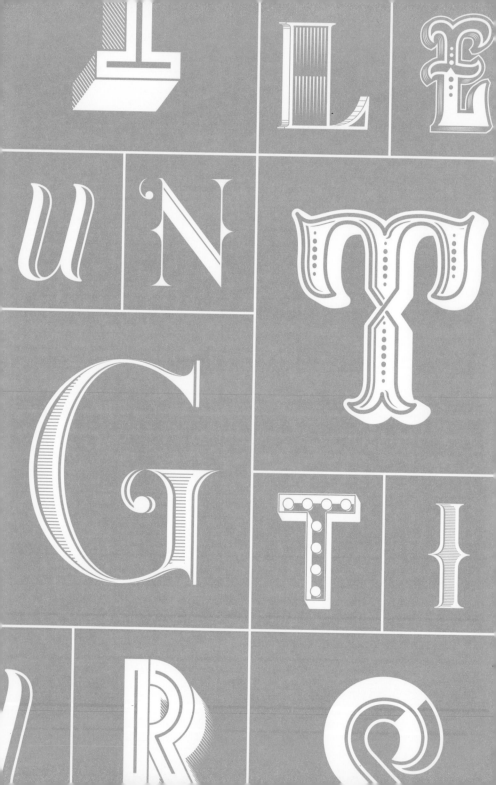